Girls Rock

Indonesia

OTHER TITLES IN
THE COLLECTION

The Wrestling Cholitas of Bolivia
The Mermaids of Jamaica
The Amazing Students of Venezuela

Written by
CLAUDIA BELLANTE

Illustrated by
JOSEFINA SCHARGORODSKY

Girls Rock

Indonesia

Crocodile Books, USA

An imprint of Interlink Publishing Group, Inc.

www.interlinkbooks.com

To Mirko: me and you, you and me.

Claudia

• • • •

For Juana, may the music always be with you.

Josefina

First American edition published 2022 by
CROCODILE BOOKS
An imprint of Interlink Publishing Group, Inc.
46 Crosby Street, Northampton, Massachusetts 01060
www.interlinkbooks.com

Library of Congress Cataloging-in-Publication Data available
ISBN 978-1-62371-808-4 • hardback

Printed and bound in Korea on forest-friendly paper
10 9 8 7 6 5 4 3 2 1

FSC
www.fsc.org
MIX
Paper | Supporting
responsible forestry
FSC® C023083

Against All Odds was born out of the desire to tell our kids real stories of children living in distant places and facing unique situations.

The series talks about everyday gestures that in certain contexts can become important, even to the point of changing the course of events, defying prejudices and clichés, and redirecting our attention to often-overlooked problems.

All of the events described in these books really happened or are currently happening. Only the protagonists are the result of the poetic license; the author wanted to protect the identities of the minors involved in these stories.

There is a country called Indonesia, so large that it extends over two continents: Asia and Oceania. Indonesia is made up of thousands of islands that hug the sea.

Hundreds of different groups of people coexist in the islands, each with its own language, religion, cuisine, clothes, and traditions. This is why their motto is *Bhinneka tunggal ika*, which means "Many, yet one."

Most of the people in Indonesia are Muslims, and many girls, teens, and women wear hijabs. There are all kinds of hijabs, in infinite colors and patterns, with wavy edges and beautiful embroidery. For the youngest of girls, there are also some with bear cub ears or petals that frame their face.

Among all these islands is Java, the heart of the country. This is where Jakarta, the capital, is located: A crowded city, where more than forty million people live. In Jakarta, cars and motorcycles flood the streets like rivers. Shopping malls are as large as cruise ships, and the heat and humidity envelop the people, making them feel like they're swimming in a pool.

At night, the skyscrapers that line the streets light up the sky, and sidewalks get filled with wagons and makeshift restaurants. They sell tropical fruit juices, meat skewers with peanut sauce, noodles, and pancakes, spreading spicy aromas and clouds of smoke through the air.

Outside the city, however, the countryside is quiet. The villages are surrounded by green mountains, tea plantations, and vast rice fields. Small colorful mosques sprout between the houses, and in the early mornings, boys and girls dressed in uniform leave their homes and run to school.

Every morning, Dewi, Kartika, and Kinara meet at the intersection of the three roads where they live. They each carry a backpack full of books and a prayer mat. At school, they study a lot, but they also learn the verses of the Qur'an to better understand their own religion.

Their parents want them to be educated according to their traditions. And for them to become an example for the whole village.

But the girls feel like something is missing from their lives. They talk about it when they get together to do their homework and secretly watch videos on YouTube. Ever since their literature teacher confessed that she'd been to a concert of a band called Metallica, the girls can't think of anything else. The image of a stadium full of people singing as one voice fills them with emotions.

After reading all the lyrics from these long haired men dressed in black, the girls believe the songs speak to them. They watch the videos nonstop, and while Dewi silently shouts so that she won't be found out, Kartika plays an air guitar with her eyes closed, and Kinara shakes her fists, striking the table with serving spoons as if she were playing a thunderous set of drums.

"It doesn't make sense to keep doing this," the girls say to one another. "If we like music and want to learn to play, we have to talk to someone, but who?" Their parents wouldn't understand, and they'd probably get mad. The right person is Pima, their literature teacher. So one day after school, the three girls find their courage and, in a whisper, tell her about their passion as if they were confessing a sin.

Pima smiles. She knew that by planting the seeds of curiosity with anecdotes of all kinds among her students, little by little a curious and restless flower would sprout. As a young girl, Pima used to play in a metal band. Her bandmates are now married or moved to other cities, but the instruments are still there, in Pima's garage. Pima lets the girls know that they are welcome to use them for practice.

And so, while their parents thought that they stayed at school in the afternoons to prepare for exams, the girls begin their long music journey. At first, they only cover songs by Metallica and other bands they admire, but as time goes on they feel the need to express their own thoughts and share their lives, so they begin to write their own lyrics.

They want to sing about school, which should leave more space for creativity; about the freedom to follow their dreams; about their religion, which is not against the music they like; their veils, which they wear because they want to, not because they're told to. Pima notices their progress; she's proud of her students and knows how talented they are, so one day, without telling them, she calls a friend of hers from Jakarta, a producer who she thinks should listen to them.

Yuka, the producer, arrives a few days later. Pima takes him to the garage and introduces him as a friend so as not to make the girls nervous. They play and sing; Yuka is impressed: "They're really good," he tells Pima. "I'd like to set up an interview for them with a local TV station and record a CD of their songs."

Dewi, Kartika, and Kinara are delighted and excited, but also worried. What if their parents find out? What if the mosque's imam, who is certainly not a lover of metal music, hears about it? And what will their classmates say, especially those who've been making fun of them for wearing leather jackets and T-shirts with their favorite band logos?

The teacher calms them down. They're not doing anything wrong. Being a good Muslim woman doesn't mean not playing in a band. They just need patience and perseverance. Finally the night of the show arrives, and the girls come up with an excuse to gather their families at Kinara's house, which has the largest TV. They carefully prepare the *nasi goreng* (fried rice, chicken, and shrimp) for everyone, and wait, holding on to one another's hands without saying a word.

The parents don't understand why their daughters are suddenly acting so polite, but they eat with pleasure. When the girls start singing onscreen, Dewi's little brother yells, "Look! Look!" Immediately, Kartika's father becomes enraged, but her mother, fascinated, calms him down. Dewi's parents involuntarily start clapping, and Kinara's mother turns the faucet off in the kitchen so she can hear better.

The next day, everyone stares at them when they leave their homes. Some people treat them like superstars, asking for selfies; others reproach them for having broken the rules of Islam.

"Who says a girl in a hijab can't play loud music?" Pima asks the girls when they tell her about the complaints.

"Does the Qur'an forbid following our dreams? The problem is that in a small town everyone knows one another, and people often criticize others for no reason. You can't let anyone get in your way; otherwise, you'll end up leaving music behind like I did."

Little by little, the criticism fades away, and one day Pima calls the girls' parents to inform them of a metal-band festival in Jakarta. It will be a unique opportunity for the girls. The parents are worried that the big city might swallow their daughters and set them on the wrong path, but they trust Pima.

The girls are dying to go. They even came up with a name for their band: Zirah, which means "armor." Music, they believe, will protect them from prejudice and radicalism. As the bus slowly leaves the village, Dewi, Kartika, and Kinara look at the sweet hills that surround their houses and promise to return soon. But for now, the city of a thousand lights awaits them, and they cannot be late for the show.

AUTHOR'S NOTE

This story arose from my curiosity about a group of young musicians from the province of Garut, in the island of Java. They are called VoB, Voice of Baceprot, which in Javanese means "noise."

Major newspapers like the *New York Times* and the *Guardian* have written about them because they play metal music, wear hijabs, and have become a symbol of women's emancipation against radical Islam.

So, relying on this narrative, I thought they'd be the perfect main characters for a book in our *Against All Odds* series. I decided to go to Indonesia.

I traveled to Jakarta in November 2019, and although I wasn't able to speak directly with the girls because they live in a remote village, I met many young women who helped me put the facts together accurately and inspire this story. Among them were journalists, activists, teachers, and the girls from Zirah, the rock group from which I borrowed the name for the band in this book. Thanks to their testimonies, I realized that in Indonesia, with the exception of a few extremist groups, Islam has always been, and continues to be, an open, modern, and tolerant religion.

Many women choose to wear the hijab. Muslim feminist groups are increasingly present in political and social scenes. These facts prove that feminism and religious modest dress are not in contradiction of each other, despite what some people in western countries mistakenly believe.

The continued relevance of VoB is that they are role models for other girls like them who want to have their own space in the still very male-dominated Indonesian music scene. And, of course, their own songs: in which young people in Indonesia—and our sons and daughters across the world—can see themselves. I want to dedicate this book to the people I met during my stay in Jakarta, a fascinating city full of possibilities: Yuka; Pima and her husband, Nino; Alma and Nikita from *Magdalene* magazine; Chika; Rika; and Anissa, Alyssa, Raissa, and Talitha from Zirah.

This book is based on a true story.
https://www.youtube.com/watch?v=AtHb-7bTOql

CLAUDIA BELLANTE